I0102344

LORD of the RING

Ethereal Power of Rings

Meredith Carson

World Codex Staff

The World Codex, LLC © 2018

PEER INTO OUR PLANET

Contents

PROLEGOMENON

"All men by nature desire to know." This Aristotelian quote from *METAPHYSICS* Book One succinctly expresses the impetus for my work on the ROPE theory. My name is John Rollins, and I too have an affinity for all things metaphysical in nature.

I am presently residing in the city of London where I was born. Here, in late October of 2016, I received an intriguing package through the post. It contained an authentic Roman ring and a detailed account of how it came to be sent to me. The contents of that package have repeatedly served as a source of inspiration in my ongoing endeavor to delve deeper into my research regarding Resonant Occultic Parapsychological Energy, or ROPE.

In a case of paramnesia or coincidence, the acronym ROPE is the exact reverse of the first letters of the following story's subtitle, *Ethereal Power of Rings*. Much to my surprise that quintessential connection is what prompted Meredith Carson, the head writer of the World Codex staff, to contact me.

In the following story, historicity is woven throughout its plot interlacing several eye-witness accounts of parapsychological phenomena that can neither be confirmed nor denied. Therefore, Lord of the Ring is categorized as Subjective Mystical Reality (SMR) which means that the perception and understanding of reality are entirely reliant upon the individual point of view of each reader.

SMR is a new literary category, and its thematic propensity reflects the incredible results of the double slit experiment in physics. In Lord of the Ring's companion book, The Shooting, the strange principles inherent to the nature of Subjective Mystical Reality are explored on several levels. In a nutshell, fact and fiction are proven to be subjective, although the appearance of the two diametrically opposed states of being has long been assumed to be understood objectively. Science has recently redefined the reality that the world experiences in everyday life. Each individual's perception of what is real may indeed be accurate.

In a professional case of quid pro quo, Miss Carson shared a bit about her experiences with SMR which intrigued me. I was impressed by her understanding of its ethereal esthetic and far-reaching metaphysical implications. SMR is very similar to ROPE in its propensity for inspiring a paradigm shift regarding perception. Both also intrinsically challenge the materialistic worldview as does Rupert Sheldrake's theory of morphic resonance.

After talking, both she and I were gobsmacked when we realized that my personal connection to this story was unbeknownst to her beforehand. Apparently, it was solely my insight into the subject matter that was paramount to her. To be more precise, certain pertinent aspects of the ROPE theory had drawn her attention and inspired her to investigate it further.

ROPE is an easy acronym to remember. More importantly, it also doubles as a metaphor for its meaning. It represents the aberrant thread which is woven throughout both time and space as it embraces a collective memory for all things, animate and inanimate alike. Such intertwined metaphysical manifestations are experienced with normal sensory perception and cognition, as well as extra-sensory perception aka ESP.

The package I received back in October of 2016 is only part of the story. It encapsulates what the World Codex staff would categorize as SMR, and I would offer as proof of ROPE; those events which occur beyond the limits and grasp of mainstream academia and the default dogmas it is adherent to. The parcel was wrapped in plain brown paper and contained an enigmatically inscribed oversized gold signet ring. Also tucked inside was a detailed first-hand account of where, when, and how the ring was found, and an insightful narrative describing several similar happenstances regarding the ethereal nature of the ring itself.

As I read the letter, it became clear that it was my responsibility to keep the ring safe until its rightful owner, Bret Bartlett, could return to London and collect it from me when he was ready to do so. In a tragic case of irony - despite the fact that he sent it to me for safekeeping - the valuable ring was stolen from my flat just one day shy of a fortnight after I had received it. As of yet, it has not been recovered. Evidently, from Bret Bartlett's perspective, there were forces at play concerning the ring that are greater than I have ever experienced before. At least that was the impression that I got as I read his letter. The "cursed" ring, as he referred to it several times, was once again stolen, just as it had been in the 4th century.

Based on previous experiences the Bartlett family was kind enough to share, you may not be surprised to learn why the ring was ultimately sent to me. For the record, I did not agree with Bret's plans for it once I read his letter. I felt as though he had unearthed it because he was meant to do so through his research, diligence, and ingenuity, and even despite his own self-doubt. Be that as it may, he planned on returning to London and burying the ring in the original spot from which it had been stolen more than 1,600 years ago.

Although Bret Bartlett's account has been embellished by Meredith Carson of the World Codex staff to produce a better-crafted story, his narrative remains the basis of the plot. In my professional opinion, the following rendering exemplifies vital elements of the three parapsychological theories mentioned above in a succinct depiction of a bizarre chain of events as it unfolded.

John Rollins, Ph.D. Metaphysics

Chapter 1: A Perfect Circle

Excerpt from Bret Bartlett's letter to John Rollins:

Dear Jack,

I hope you get this letter and enclosed ring without incident first of all. The way things have been going, I wouldn't be surprised if there was a plane crash because of my attempt to send it to you, but as no one else was aware of the contents, I figured it would be ok. I wanted to tell you many things about what I did, and what I feel resulted from my meddling in circumstances that I might have been wiser to avoid. As you probably are well aware by now, I ignored the advice you gave me…which I now regret.

Sometimes my curious nature gets the best of my judgment. I have to believe that it is partly my father's fault. He started me thinking about things in an odd out of body kind of manner, as though I was somehow inherently protected, and I want to tell you how that came about before I delve into my own experience with the ring you are probably now holding. Please don't put the ring around your finger!

Maybe if I explain why I feel the need to distance myself from the ring that I unearthed - by sending it back to the country where I found it - you will gain some insight beyond the limits of my own understanding. I want to tell you this story first so you can see what I mean about my father's influence.

When I was young, I asked my father why he and my mother got divorced. To this day I'm not sure why he told me the story that he did, but it is true, every word. I know it must have had something to do with the reasons why they didn't stay married, at least as far as he was concerned.

He said that one summer, he, his brother, and a friend, had all taken the ferry over to Martha's Vineyard for the day, to explore a little, and go swimming on South Beach. To make a long story short, my mother didn't go with them as they were not getting along well at the time. He had his wedding ring on as always, and he emphasized to me that he never took it off while they were married.

My father is a good swimmer. While he was at the beach, he went into the ocean for a swim, but the

*tide and waves were making it hard to reach the beach
once he had swum out a way. He was beginning to
feel fatigued when he wisely decided to come back to
shore and rest. As he was slowly making progress
toward the beach, he realized that the tide had pulled
him out further than he had thought. He began to
swim with much greater determination - when all at
once his wedding band slid down his finger - right to
the very tip.*

*He quickly closed his hand, trapping the ring
inside of his fist, subsequently saving it from being lost
in the ocean. Within a minute or two he became
cognizant of the fact that attempting to swim efficiently
with one hand closed is nearly impossible. He had no
pockets in his swim trunks, and couldn't hold it in his
mouth for fear of choking. While he worked hard
swimming into shore, he quickly recognized that he
was caught in a double-bind. He could not make it
into the beach while he was holding on to the wedding
ring.*

*He said that he was already too tired to fight and
try to hold on to the ring because he was beginning to
fear that he wouldn't reach the shore at the pace he
was moving. So, he let the ring out of his hand and
swam as hard as he could to avoid drowning in the*

ocean. As it was, he said that he barely made it in and collapsed on the beach, thoroughly exhausted.

That was a little less than six months before my parents got divorced. He told me that the way things happened it became evident to him that the act of releasing the ring into the ocean to survive was an omen. The marriage had ended, and things had to happen just as they did, perhaps as a way of illustrating the point.

With all that has happened to my brother and me since then, I understand better that rationalization. I've never shared that story with anyone other than you. I know that you find that kind of metaphor as a thread between realities fascinating.

As an entirely bizarre coincidence, after my father and I moved to Florida, ten years or so later, we were walking along the beach near Daytona when something Déjà vu like occurred.

We were talking and walking along a long stretch of beach away from the crowd. We were minding our own business when an old woman approached us out of nowhere. She pointed out toward the ocean and made a note of the size of the waves. Then she emphatically attempted to convey that the people who were making loud sounds about 150 feet out in the surf were no doubt in trouble. As my father and I looked out across the surface of the water, we thought they were just having fun and assured the old lady that there was no problem. We shrugged off the encounter and continued walking along the beach.

After only a few more steps, she hurried up to us again and exclaimed, "No, no, I think they are drowning! LOOK!" We quickly assessed that she was right, and without any more hesitation, we dove into the water after them. It was an African American man, and his two children, and they were drowning just as the woman had indicated. The three of them reminded me of my father, my brother, and I, and it became clear that they were being sucked out by the riptide and would perish if we didn't rescue them.

My father managed to reach them first, and he pulled in both kids, just enough for me to grab them and get them safely back to the beach. Their teeth were chattering, not from cold, but with fear because of the shock they were in. The look on their frightened faces I have never since forgotten.

My father swam as fast as he could after the guy who was further out and moving away. The guy was big, but fortunately, when my dad got within five or six feet of him, a lifeguard came swimming up fast behind him. He tapped my father on the shoulder to take over, and he saved the guy with a rescue board. Just like the old woman, the lifeguard seemed to appear out of nowhere.

Later my father shared with me that he had his doubts about being able to bring that big guy back to shore by himself. The rescue board made it so easy for the lifeguard to do the job. The success of the rescue was nothing short of miraculous.

When we were all safely back on the beach and had calmed down some, they thanked us both. We told them that it was, in fact, the old woman who had saved their lives, and without her, they would have drowned. At first, we were adamant that they were in no danger, but her insistence made us pay closer attention to the situation.

All of us scanned the beach, yet the old woman was gone. She had disappeared during the commotion and was nowhere to be found afterward. My father and I were the only ones who saw her, not even the lifeguard did. Apparently, she disappeared during all the excitement - it was a bit bizarre the way she just vanished.

About fifteen minutes later, as my father and I were walking away from the spot where we had fished those people out of the ocean, he noticed something shiny in the sand. A reflected glimmer of the sun had caught his eye, and he reached down and retrieved its source. It turned out to be a man's gold wedding band. He swished it around in the water and then slipped it onto his finger just to see if it fit. Again, because he had no pockets, he wore it until he got back home. He still has that ring to this day. It fit him perfectly.

Chapter 2: Melting Memories

A little less than a decade earlier, in shoe city, better known as Brockton Massachusetts, that same working man, Scott Bartlett, and his two sons experienced what many people speculate about but only a rare few ever experience first-hand. Through providence or fate, they were thrust into a world of shadow. It was a world of shadow not created from a desire for power, or ambition, but only brought into focus through an innate vigilance on their behalf which lent a heightened level of awareness of such a realm.

Statistically, it seems that only a select few are gifted with the ability to see into that world of shadows and hazy twilight through their very own eyes. In the Bartlett's case, perhaps it was a family trait. When Scott was younger, his mother used to joke with him that their propensity for foresight was due to their Native American heritage. Her grandmother was a full-blooded Penobscot from northern Maine. Henry David Thoreau had romanticized the Indian way of life and their close connection with the natural world. He was a frequent visitor to the Penobscot villages, and when he was on his deathbed, his last dying word was reported to be "Indian."

In a much similar way, as it was in J.R.R. Tolkien's life, and in his novels, there are those who sense power which transcends time. In Tolkien's case, he focused in on the power of the machine which he attributed to a device more commonly accepted as the ring. In the following account, it appears as though foresight and power collaborated in a concerted effort to bend reality - just as the light from a storm filters through dark clouds and bends to produce a vivid rainbow.

Out of a clear blue sky, a windfall of twenty thousand dollars fell into Scott's lap in October of 1990 when his wealthy aunt met an untimely demise and bequeathed the money to him. The timing couldn't have been more perfect for that amount of cash because he had been hoping to purchase a house in Brockton, where at that time the housing market was very affordable. He had been working hard to save up enough for the down payment, and now that he had it in hand he began to shop around in search of a good bargain.

Within just a couple of days, he found precisely what he was looking for. It was a fixer-upper not more than five minutes from his work. The best part about it was that it was listed for only 50,000 dollars.

The neighborhood was perfect for a busy place like Brockton. The house was situated on a decent sized, quiet corner lot. The small street that ran parallel to the main road was a dead end on either side, so there was no thru traffic. Riverside drive passed by the house and at its end, just a short distance away, sat a small quiet park used only intermittently for little league baseball practice. Because there were no bleachers for an audience, the small quiet park was pretty much an out of the way and overlooked idyllically serene spot.

At the other end of the street was a forgotten dry riverbed that wasn't even noticeable from the road as you passed by. Less than two years earlier there was a dead body found in that overgrown river bed, not more than a hundred yards or so from the house. That's part of the reason why the asking price was so low, and Scott took advantage of that fact. He was initially unaware of any other reasons for the reduced amount, but he learned them all too soon during his fact-finding mission.

Caveat emptor was something he fully embraced - yet sometimes the best-laid plans of mice and men often go awry - despite our best intentions. Before he decided to make an offer on the house, he resolved to knock on the door of the nearest neighbor whose home was also coincidentally for sale. The next door neighbor's house was more impressive, but it was listed for 60,000 dollars. It wasn't a corner lot which made him vacillate a bit between the two. So he decided to have a look inside in an attempt to help make up his mind.

After he formulated a friendly greeting, he knocked on the neighbor's front door. He waited a minute or so until a frail-looking grey-haired old woman sheepishly peeked through the sidelight. He peered inside the house as the door slowly opened. Immediately, he was struck by the stacks of old newspapers and bags full of stuff that looked like it may have been trash. It was piled up everywhere, except for a well-worn pathway which to him appeared much like a maze.

The next thing that he noticed before either of them spoke a word was an odd pungent odor emanating from across the threshold. In that instant, that first impression, he made up his mind and knew that the other house was what he wanted beyond any shadow of a doubt.

So as not to seem like he was wasting the woman's time, he politely introduced himself and then informed her that he was interested in buying the house next door to hers. She awkwardly announced that her name was Ruth - as she conveyed that information there seemed to be an odd gleam in her eye - yet it went unaddressed for the moment. At that point, he had only planned on making a bit of small talk, but her response to his first question took him wholly by surprise.

"How is the neighborhood here?" He smiled. The woman seemed a bit puzzled by the innocuous question. She responded, "The neighborhood is fine, but that's not the problem."

"Oh, what is the problem?" He waited patiently as she seemed to contemplate how to best phrase her thoughts, and convey them as delicately as possible, but then in a lackadaisical manner she just blurted them out.

"The problem is that ever since my father found that woman in the bathtub with both of her wrists slit, the house next door has been haunted by her ghost. I can only assume that is why you're here - to buy that house - or perhaps this one."

Not to be dissuaded by an old woman's superstitions, Scott did nonetheless become curious, "How long ago was that? A dark countenance seemed to pass across her careworn and wrinkled face as a glazed look came into her eyes. Like a haze which carried memories from her past. It forced her to cast her distant stare downward with a sense of loss and despair. Then she offered what felt like a chilling soliloquy.

"I was only eleven…just eleven. It still feels like yesterday. Sarah's body was being carried out of the house with a bloody sheet draped over her. The wind was whipping up, and it blew the sheet from off of her face as the two men were sliding the stretcher into the back of the ambulance. That was the last time I ever saw her face. My father was watching helplessly as he stood there on the front lawn. He seemed to be struggling to hold back his tears, but all that he was able to do was wipe them with his sleeve as they fell. We couldn't look away, neither one of us."

The heartbroken old woman composed herself a little, and then she suddenly glanced back up and spoke directly to him.

"Just before the doors closed and the ambulance drove away, I saw her hand slip down off of the stretcher. I remember thinking that she was waving goodbye to me for the last time. I've had nightmares about it off and on, and sometimes she cries at night when the silence becomes too deafening. She sobs terribly even now. If you buy that house, you will hear her."

Without saying another word, Ruth did an about-face and shuffled back inside of her home. She meandered through the mess that had sadly culminated into a life that she was now looking forward to departing. With the front door still open, like some kind of portal into the past, Scott watched as she disappeared out of sight for a few moments. He stood there on her porch waiting and wondering what to do. Then he pensively peered over at the house that he was about to purchase, all the while being more than a little bit vexed by the question running around in his mind. Was her story real or only imagined?

He began to think that the old woman may merely be lonely and need companionship, someone kind enough to occasionally come and visit with her. Just then, after working her way back through the labyrinth of her life's leftovers, she appeared once again at the door carrying an old worn, dusty book. She opened it and then carefully pulled out a yellowed, handwritten piece of paper. Holding it in her frail trembling hand, she began to speak softly, almost as though she were once again thinking out loud.

"My dad took this poem from beside Sarah's body before the police came. For him, it seemed to hold a great deal of significance and meaning. He kept it safe, and I have held on to it for all these years since his passing. My father was killed in a robbery attempt three days before my 13th birthday. I was informed by the police that it was a case of just being in the wrong place at the wrong time.

According to his account of things my mother had died giving birth to me - yet he only ever shared very few details about her - which always made me think he was hiding something.

Sarah Gooden was the name of the woman who lived next door, and in my memories, she has a warm heart, like that of a good friend instead of just a neighbor. She was fun and generous to me when I was a little girl. I guess that's partly why my father was so upset when she committed suicide. I can recall that on one occasion, shortly before her death, he shared his opinion of her with me. He told me that she was an eccentric and fanciful woman. Then he softened his expression and followed that criticism up with this sentiment, 'She was both kind and beautiful.'

Many times since his passing, I've wondered why it was he who had discovered her upstairs in the bathtub that horrible day. I still ponder what the truth may be, but I guess I'll never know while I'm still lingering on this earth."

As if she were somehow expecting Scott to help ease her lifelong lament, she smiled at him in a way that evoked more than a modicum of empathy. To his surprise, she then placed her precious piece of paper in his hand. As he took it, there was a brief instant where he almost gave it back to her without reading it. It felt to him as though he were intruding, much like peeking into a private world that was none of his business. For a second he got the feeling he might be better off if he resisted that temptation. Then reconsidering, he thought to himself - if I do end up buying the house - maybe I am supposed to read it after all. So he did.

MELTING MEMORIES

Empress, temptress, pulling strings for finer things —

Envoy to a Ruth-less queen…

Breaking hearts of impish upstarts —

Bordering on the obscene.

Washing and scrubbing with bleach and lye —

To repent as I come clean;

Trapped in a world of do or die,

For I will not rest between…

Do or die, stay or fly; only I must choose,

Conceal the sin — cease or begin —

Will I cry? – If I win – or lose?

My melting memories and dreams disappear,

Softly trickling down the drain –

To imagine the cruel sound of things they will say;

Plagues my boiling brain,

Yet I'm cooled by the pooling water –

Like a sweet soft summer rain…

Posed in a picture of gory pity;

As I pass through this portal of pain.

Where the only glory of my story is this –

I am sad, mad, and insane…

Chapter 3: A Deal, A Dream, & A Death

After being bothered by the ghost story that the curious old woman had told him, and juxtaposed with the musty and dusty condition of her home, Scott finally made up his mind about which purchase to make. Friday, after he got home from work, he perused the newspaper one last time, and then made the call. He had decided to try and strike a deal concerning the price of the house on the corner lot. He felt like he had a pretty good advantage knowing the backstory of the property now – and he surmised that because it was vacant - it was obviously unwanted by the owner.

A young guy answered the phone. He and Scott talked for a few minutes about the ideal location of the house on the corner. That context enabled Scott to cleverly shift the conversation in his favor. He brought up the fact that a dead body was found just at the end of the street a couple years earlier. The current homeowner attempted to convey that it was not something relevant to the quality of the neighborhood, but he eventually conceded that it had been a deterrent in the sale of the house thus far.

Scott informed him that he had spoken to the old woman who lived next door and that she had expressed concerns of her own regarding the house. The homeowner got very quiet, almost as though he were holding his breath momentarily. Scott presented the idea that maybe the old house was haunted just to see what kind of reaction he would get. The price was already low at 50,000 dollars so he knew that there must be a pretty good reason why.

For about ten seconds there was silence on the other end of the phone. Then the homeowner said, "To be honest, I think the woman next door is away with the fairies. As far as I know, the house is just an ordinary old house, and it's still in pretty good condition too."

Scott had already peeked inside the windows of every room downstairs and could see that it was in decent condition even though it was outdated, dark, and drabby. It only had one bathroom, and there was no shower, but it had three bedrooms. Wheels of providence were already in motion as the two of them continued bargaining.

"The reason it is listed for such a good price is because I inherited it a few years back, but I don't like Brockton much, and I'm closer to Boston where I am now. The back taxes are beginning to add up, and I just want to let it go in a quick sale."

That was it! Scott saw the opportunity he needed to lowball the guy and see if he could get the knee-jerk reaction he had been hoping for.

"I just got the money I need for the down payment and some of the remodeling, but the price is too high for me. If you can let it go for less, then we can make a deal and get it done." Again several long seconds passed, followed by the homeowner's weak rebuttal.

"How much money are we talking about?"

"Thirty-two thousand dollars is what I want to spend on that house. The roof needs to be re-shingled right away. I have to remove and replace that old shed in the backyard, and I need to put another bathroom in just for starters."

Scott waited patiently as he anticipated the counteroffer. He was trying hard not to expect to close the deal for that ridiculously low price. The response he got took him entirely by surprise.

"Ok, I can do it for that much." The two men discussed some superfluous information, and that was it. Scott left his phone number with the guy just in case there were any unforeseen problems. About three hours later, after he had eaten supper and was about to go out, the phone rang.

The caller was an older guy, seemingly earnest in his demeanor. He introduced himself as the father of the owner of the house who Scott had spoken with earlier. He informed Scott that after looking at his son's money situation more closely and considering the back taxes he had incurred, unfortunately, his son would be financially forced to back out of the verbal agreement. The older and wiser gentleman genuinely seemed to be apologetic about it. Scott just listened and let him express his thoughts until he was through with his spiel which was apparently aimed at evoking a sympathetic counter offer.

Because he had started with such a low amount, and it had almost worked, Scott responded with the same story. "I need to put a lot of money and time into fixing it up. It needs another bathroom which means pretty much all the plumbing will have to be updated. I can't offer much more than what I told your son earlier. However, the most I can do to make it work for me is 36,500 dollars."

The polite gentlemen chuckled quietly, paused for a moment and then capitulated. "Ok, it's a deal." Scott was satisfied because he felt that striking a deal where both sides can walk away from the bargaining table happy is how business should be conducted. At that instant, as the deal was struck, strange and inexplicable events were set into motion that nobody could have ever anticipated.

Six months had passed, and Scott and his two sons were staying in the house occasionally while he worked on some aspects of the interior remodeling. He was concentrating on the removal of the old pantry. When he was finished, it would be completely converted into a full bathroom, including a tub/shower, toilet, and sink. He had already removed the old iron claw-footed tub from the small upstairs bathroom where the woman was found dead. That was one of the first things he did when he took possession of the house.

In the process of remodeling, he came across some old newspapers and a few old books too. He found a valuable early edition of the Wizard of Oz, an old poetry magazine from Boston, plus a very old publication about the witchcraft trials in Salem. A friend from work told him it was probably a grimoire or book of shadows. Scott didn't want the books to get accidentally thrown away or ruined somehow, so he moved them to a somewhat less chaotic atmosphere while he was remodeling. He stored them at his parents' house for safekeeping.

That decision turned out to be a good one. One day, not long after, while he was at work, a massive thunderstorm hit Brockton with very little warning.

It was later reported to have been a rear flank downdraft, or RFD, aka a supercell. It came complete with golf-ball sized hail, and there were even reports of a funnel cloud. The sky turned an ominous green hue which rarely ever happens in that part of the country.

The violent downforce of the wind had ripped off part of the roof and bent the metal support for the gutter next to the electrical power line supplying Scott's house. This happened in the early afternoon while he was busy at work only a few miles away. Fortunately, both of his sons were nowhere near the house at the time of the storm. They were spending the day with their mother helping out with some volunteer work at the homeless shelter in downtown Brockton.

Before Scott had left work that day, his father had called him to ask if he would come and help him remove a big fallen tree limb that had landed in the driveway during the storm. All the while, he had no idea of the damage that had occurred at his own place. Scott was afraid to go look because he had a bad feeling. So he decided to stay with his parents for the night and put it off for just one more day. He never really understood the saying, "a stitch in time, saves nine," but very soon he would come to appreciate exactly what it means.

While he was sleeping that night, he slipped into a volatile dream state. He awoke from his sleep in a daze, and it took him a few moments to realize that he was only dreaming. As a result of the realism he had invented in his mind's eye during the dream, he had a bizarre somnambulistic reaction. He had awakened clutching his car keys in his hand. Nothing like that had ever happened to him before, and after which he felt compelled to go check out his house to make sure that everything was ok.

By then it was almost 3:30 in the morning, so he quietly got up and got dressed. The drive was just shy of fifteen minutes without any traffic. He stealthily snuck out to check out his place because now his curiosity was beginning to gnaw at his peace of mind. As he drew closer to his destination - he was struck by a sinking feeling - an ominous sense of dread had taken hold over him.

When he reached Riverside Drive, he pulled his car over right next to the spot where that body had been found a few years back. The road ahead was blocked by firetrucks, police cars, and an ambulance. He almost choked from the thick smoke enveloping his car, so he rolled his window up tightly. His house was engulfed in flames, and there was nothing he could do at that moment but watch it burn. He sat silently defeated for several minutes hypnotized by the eerie orange glow flickering against the black sky. If there really was a hellfire he thought to himself – then this was it - it seemed to be enjoying the violent manner by which it was destroying all of his plans with its purposeful intensity.

What hadn't been revealed to him in his dream was that the house next door to his was also ablaze. The magnitude of the fire was consuming both structures. In a brief moment of clarity, he realized that the two houses had always been intertwined and were simultaneously being purged of their existence forever. Both houses which had held secrets for years were now being reduced to nothing more than a pile of rubble and ash. He could envision the enigmatic old woman now. He saw the image of her charred corpse flashing in his mind like a neon sign. Somewhere - lost inside of the maze that she had created - she had become trapped and then burned alive. He struggled to put that horrifying vision out of his mind.

As Scott rolled the driver's window back down, he drove away into the darkness. While he was driving, he was thinking about how ironic it was that he had removed the old books for safekeeping. That was the only upside to this tragedy that came to mind at that moment. He kept those books and other important things in a steel lockbox in his bedroom, and he felt the need to visit them briefly before resigning himself to going back to bed. When he reached his parent's house, he sat in the driveway until he worked up enough desire to go inside. He was right back where he had started, and that reality check felt like a slap in the face.

Scott retrieved the box from his closet and opened it. It smelled like there had been a fire inside of it. He attributed that sensation to his imagination considering the circumstances. He methodically removed the contents which included the old newspapers, the Wizard of Oz book, and the poetry magazine. He was stunned when he realized that the book about witchcraft was missing. Then a few seconds later, he realized that in its place at the bottom of the box was a small pile of black ashes. He never closed his eyes again that night - for fear of dreaming.

Arson investigators later concluded that the devastating fire started because of damage to the roof that had resulted from the violent downdraft earlier in the day. The twisted and bent metal gutter support shorted out the old wiring when it made contact with the downed power line to the house. They said it was a fluke, but it wreaked havoc with the antiquated fuse box. The wet wood from the rain had smoldered for hours after the storm before the initial combustion had ignited into flames. With that news, Scott knew that his procrastination had cost him his investment. He also became aware that if he had gone to his house first, before heading to his parent's place, he might have been able to save Ruth from her tragic fate.

Chapter 4: Brink of Discovery

Fifteen years had passed since that horrible fire in Brockton happened. On a positive note, two weeks after the fire Scott learned that the old Wizard of Oz book he had found was a signed first edition copy, and it was very rare. Because the book was in such good condition, he was offered 15,000 dollars from a reputable book dealer in Boston. He took the money.

Scott's older son Bret, after high school, enlisted in the navy. His younger son Oliver was still living in shoe city with his mother. They lived just down the street from where his old house had stood, but both lots were empty now. Scott had eventually moved to Florida to escape the long New England winters, and everything that had transpired was all but forgotten.

The autumn leaves were reaching their colorful peak as they always do early in October in the Boston area. On a crisp, chilly New England fall day, Oliver could find little to do except to relax and take it easy. He was tired because he had spent the better part of the previous day, Saturday, playing baseball in that little park adjacent to Riverside Dr. The fresh air and exercise made it too hard to resist spending as much time as possible outdoors during the last days of good weather. The amount of boredom that sometimes begins to settle in when the gloominess of winter approaches in New England is best compensated for by sunshine.

Sunday was Oliver's day to unwind from both his school and work. It gave him a chance to rest from playing ball. As an ancillary benefit, around supper time, he picked up a fresh, hot, Margherita pizza from the place he frequented down the street from his mother's house. Continuing to live with his mother after high school helped him conserve his funds. He was happy to be able to afford pizza, an occasional date, and a beater box to drive, as he liked to refer to it.

Having the whole house to himself was often the case on a lazy Sunday afternoon. He commenced his usual perusal of the movie listings on television, and after some considerable effort, he stumbled across a movie channel with no mind-numbing commercials. The movie that was about to begin was *The Fellowship of the Ring*, based on the book by J.R.R. Tolkien. He reclined on the couch with his feet up to get more comfortable as the movie began.

Oliver's eyelids started to get heavy. His mind wandered a bit remembering a strange thing that he had experienced while he was staying with his father in that old house, just before it burned down. He was a little boy at the time, and the tale he told his father back then was presumed to be the result of a child's overactive imagination. Even his brother Bret didn't believe him at first.

The idea of a ring possessing supernatural powers, as depicted in the movie, made him recall the details of what he experienced all those years ago. He tried hard to focus on the film and not to give in to the temptation of remembering the frightening event, but it had recently been on his mind. A month or so earlier, Oliver had been matriculated into a degree program at his college, and he was assigned to write an essay about any story of his choosing from the last century, instead of the earlier works most typically focused on. The idea was to try and bring to light the subtext and some of the thematic images that were slightly beneath the plot line and may be relatable to the world we are living in now. With an IQ of 140, when Oliver Bartlett applied his mind, he displayed a unique ability to glean details that may escape those following along with the flow of the story solely for its entertainment value.

He had watched *The Fellowship of the Ring* before, but he had never taken the time to read the book. He began to get curious about the comparisons between the two vastly different mediums. As the movie progressed, he got an idea. He decided to turn off the television and see if he could find a copy of the book and read it from cover to cover.

His goal was to try and compare and contrast the differences between the movie and the book. By doing that, he planned on drawing a more accurate picture of what he believed the thematic nature of the story is. Through closer examination and scrutiny, he hoped to find more poignant metaphors and similes poised and ready to pop off the pages of the book. Some, no doubt, would also be subtly hidden between the lines.

With almost two weeks to complete the assignment, he had plenty of time. If he wasn't mistaken, he was reasonably sure that his brother had a copy of the book since they both were fans of the movie trilogy. Oliver made the quantum leap of assuming that the book might still be somewhere in Bret's old room. Bret was currently living in Connecticut after serving in military intelligence in London. His old room still had many of his things left in it, including some of his books.

Oliver rummaged through some of the books that were in a bookcase by Bret's bed but didn't find what he was looking for. That would have been much too easy he thought to himself, as he sat on the edge of the bed contemplatively. For a quick second, he even considered calling his brother, but he didn't want to be a nuisance concerning something so trivial. So he decided to turn it into a scavenger hunt, a personal challenge. He tried to picture where it might be based on what he knew about his brother.

His brother Bret was a private person, overtly gregarious, but innately introverted. He too had a genius IQ which manifested itself occasionally in his competitiveness, usually in instances of healthy sibling rivalry. Bret had scored very highly on his Armed Services Vocational Aptitude Battery (ASVAB) and then finished at the top of his class in military intelligence training. Shortly after which he began living and working in London. In his downtime, he enjoyed exploring England's historically fascinating culture and green pastoral countryside as often as he could.

While he was there, he also managed to delve into a bit of personal research regarding J.R.R. Tolkien, although he was tight-lipped about it. Even as a young boy he was fascinated by Tolkien's style and the preponderance of creativity necessary to so adequately embellish the themes that are conveyed throughout his work. It was kind of ironic that his brother was now beginning to do the exact same thing. If it weren't for the essay that Oliver had become intent about writing, perhaps that connection between the two brothers would never have been realized.

Bret had been in the navy and stationed in London for about thirteen months, but for some unknown reason he was granted an early discharge from his service and came back to the US. Shortly after which he enrolled in college and began to take an interest in antiquities and rare artifacts. The more obscure they were, the more he seemed to be interested in what secrets they might reveal. Upon closer inspection, he began to appreciate the depth and context of the backstory that each inevitably held when sufficiently researched.

To that end, he told his family and friends that he was studying to be an antiquarian. At the time, however, none of it made too much sense to his brother or his father. Bret was never easily influenced or dissuaded. He had always dedicated his energy to exploring whatever captured his imagination, and became resolute and decisive when he discovered his affinity for antiquities. When asked about his sudden change of plans and circumstance, all he would say about it was that when he was in England, he had an epiphany. That simple statement raised more questions than it did to provide any satisfactory answers.

As it turns out, Bret later shared that during one of his excursions, while visiting a place called Silchester in Hampshire, he experienced what he called an "awakening." Through his ability to think outside of the box - just the way his brother was attempting to do now as he searched for the lost Tolkien book - Bret had discovered something mystical and incredible.

Chapter 5: Oliver's Nightmare

Bret's fascination with Tolkien's work was a big part of the reason why Oliver decided to write his essay about the book in the first place. He was still attempting to locate the book in Bret's old room but came up empty-handed. After about forty-five minutes of fruitlessly searching, it dawned on him that he was probably looking in the wrong place all along.

Bret's favorite place to read and to do some writing was in the backyard of his mother's house. It was big and quiet, and there was a small creek that ran along its edge, providing a calming natural boundary. Bret would sit outside quietly for hours, musing and jotting down ideas. He would write his thoughts in a worn black and white notebook that he kept, much like a journal. That was something he started doing while he was staying with his father in that old house, chronicling many of the strange occurrences as they happened.

It dawned on Oliver that he never saw that notebook in Bret's room while he was looking for the Tolkien book, and that's when he got an idea that had escaped him entirely until just that second. There was an old concrete birdbath sitting on a piece of slate in the yard near where Bret used to relax, and write. Looking out of the bedroom window and into the yard, Oliver's wheels began to spin. He ran downstairs to call Bret on the phone - mostly to test a theory he was entertaining - also not to do any unnecessary digging or heavy lifting. Oliver had the sneaking suspicion that physical work was going to be part of the quest he had begun almost an hour ago, but he was more determined now than ever to find what he was after.

The first thing Oliver said to his brother when he answered the phone was, "I found your notebook."

Bret reacted calmly, "No you didn't."

Oliver chuckled, "You're right, I didn't. How could you be so sure?" Bret laughed a bit louder.

"Because if you had really found my notebook, you would be much more emphatic about it."

"Why's that?"

Bret informed his brother that what was inside the notebook was a secret, and it could very well be inherently dangerous. He did his best to convince Oliver that if he went after it, he might be sorry he found it. That bit of new information only served to intrigue his brother all the more.

Bret told Oliver that he would come home from Connecticut the next weekend, and tell him the whole story, but made him promise not to search for the notebook in the meantime. Oliver reluctantly surrendered to his older brother's wishes.

Before they hung up, Oliver said, "Oh yeah, I almost forgot, where is your copy of *The Fellowship of the Ring*?"

"I lost it in England."

That news punctuated Oliver's quest to find the book. He was now satisfied enough to go buy his own copy.

After the brief but enlightening phone call with his brother, Oliver decided to buy the book and read it in the same place that Bret used to sit and think, and sometimes write. He quickly found that reading outside appeared to intensify the experience. Oliver got lost in the landscape of the book, visualizing the imaginative characters and places that Tolkien so vividly described.

It was Wednesday, and Oliver was already done reading more than half the book. He was looking forward to Bret's arrival in a couple of days, and he found that although he enjoyed the experience of reading outdoors, his thoughts kept drifting backward. He wondered about whatever it was that Bret said was so dangerous and was stashed in his notebook. It vexed him that he had apparently kept it so well hidden right under his nose.

Time passed quickly as Oliver engrossed himself in chapter after chapter of *The Fellowship of the Ring*, completely immersing himself in the story. Before he knew it, while he was out in the backyard reading, his brother snuck up silently and tapped him on the shoulder. They said hello and started talking, and soon they were on the subject of the book which was still in Oliver's hands. It was almost sunset by then.

A few minutes later Oliver subtly switched gears and asked his brother, "Well, are you gonna get your notebook?"

"First, tell me where you think it is."

"I think it's right here underneath the bird bath, in a box or something."

Bret smiled devilishly, "Come with me."

The two of them entered the house and then proceeded upstairs to Oliver's bedroom.

Oliver asked, "What are you doing now?"

"Watch!" Bret smirked as he got down on his knees and reached his hand up under Oliver's bed.

In just a second he produced the notebook in question, and then said, "Take this, and open it up carefully."

He handed it to his brother. Before Oliver opened the notebook, he could feel the impression of something hard pressed in between its pages. He looked at his brother with a puzzled expression because he was beginning to suspect what it could be.

"Go ahead, take it out and look at it."

"What is it?"

"You probably already know deep down don't you…"

Oliver opened the notebook to the pages where the mysterious item had been safely pressed between for more than a decade.

"It's an engagement ring…where did you find it?"

"You helped me find it when you were a little kid, you just never knew it."

"What do you mean?" Oliver began to get chills as the hair on the back of his neck stood up.

"Read the pages that describe the nightmare you had that night in dad's old house, I wrote it all down when you were telling us about it because that same night I heard a woman's voice crying and it woke me up."

"I don't have to read it, I can still see that disturbing image in my mind, and hear her voice, even now. I haven't told anyone, but I still have nightmares about her once in a while."

"Tell me again what happened that night, and I'll tell you where I found the ring."

Oliver cradled the platinum engagement ring in his ever-so-slightly trembling hand and gazed into the diamond as though it were a crystal ball. He could envision in his minds-eye precisely what had horrified him all those years ago. Haunted by the aberration that had become seared into his memory - in a low soft voice he described it with a strange perspicacity - as though it happened yesterday.

"I was asleep when I heard what sounded like a woman sobbing. Her crying woke me up, and it seemed like it was coming from the upstairs bathroom. So I sat up for a second, thinking about what I should do, and then I got out of bed. I knew that there was only me, you and dad in the house. There were no lights on. Only the dim illumination of the moonlight was filtering through the small window at the top of the stairs, making the hallway barely navigable. I didn't want to wake up anyone else and get into trouble, so I didn't turn on any lights.

Quietly, I climbed the stairs, and when I reached the bathroom door, I cautiously turned the cold brass knob and peered inside. As I took a step across that threshold, I immediately noticed a change in temperature, and then I felt my sock begin soaking up water like a sponge. The old claw-footed bathtub was filled to the top with abstruse dark water that had spilled over onto the floor. I couldn't tell what color it was, but when I looked closer, I began to see through it and caught a glimpse of something just beneath its surface. I must have given my eyes enough time to adjust although it was still difficult to conceptualize what I was witnessing. It appeared to be a face with its eyes open - staring upward - just underneath the surface of the dark pool.

As I stood there transfixed, and wondering if I was dreaming, the woman in the tub lurched suddenly from out of the water, sat up straight, and spoke to me. It was at that second that I could tell there was blood mixed in with the water, and it horrified me how it slowly started dripping down her face. In the moonlight, it looked like she was crying black tears. I became momentarily mesmerized by the sight of her and couldn't run. I just stood there frozen. I'll never forget that eerie image, and what happened next.

With her eyes wide she pleaded, 'Help me, please! I'm searching for my ring so that my daughter Ruth and I can rest in peace - I've lost my ring - Please help me find it!'

I ran back to bed but couldn't sleep the rest of the night. I just kept my eyes closed and waited for daybreak to come and rescue me from the darkness. The next morning, dad did his best to convince me that I was just dreaming, and to be honest, I wasn't really sure about it either. Although at breakfast, he had no explanation as to why one of my socks was damp."

"The story you told back then scared me too. Oliver, do you remember when dad was replacing the cast iron drain pipes from that upstairs bathroom after he threw out the old tub?"

"Yes, that was not long after I had that vision, nightmare, or whatever it was. I do remember that now."

"One day, I went down into the cellar and poked around by myself before dad got home. I was just kind of fishing for anything that might have possibly gotten trapped in the old pipes. Right before dad threw them out into the dumpster with that old tub - I found the ring! It was caught in an elbow of the old original cast iron drain pipe. Two days later, dad's house and the old lady's house next door were both burned up in the fire that happened after that big storm."

Oliver was dumbstruck for several minutes. Then he uttered this summation, "I don't think that it was a fluke accidental fire that supposedly killed that old woman. It was some kind of otherworldly funeral pyre. I'll bet that she was already dead, days before the fire even started, and no one even noticed."

Oliver then handed the notebook back his brother. Bret said to him, "Listen to this, I figured it out from that old book about witches dad found in the house when he began remodeling."

At this point, Oliver Bartlett wasn't sure he wanted to hear anymore, yet his curiosity once again got the better of him.

"Ok, what is it? Tell me!"

"Do you remember that there was a strange poem inside the back cover of that book?"

"Yes, I do."

Bret composed himself a bit and then began to read aloud from his notes.

WITCH HUNT

Yesterday, today, tomorrow - three

Past, present, future - three

Memories remembered, then forgot - naught

1661, twice as many lives undone -

As many years hence - comes the setting of the sun...

"Now listen...listen to this. Naught means wicked, but it also means zero in old English. Three, three, zero equals 330; those numbers are at the end of the first three lines. Then *1661, twice as many lives undone*; during that year the Great Scottish Witch Hunt took place and supposedly 660 people were murdered for diabolism or witchcraft."

"Wow, that's just bizarre."

"Wait till you hear the rest. It blew my mind when I figured it all out. The last line of the poem is; *As many years hence - comes the setting of the sun*. If you add 330 to 1661, you get 1991, and when you flip the years over, they are the same. 1991 was the year that dad's house and the old lady's house burned to the ground together. I think that means the witch hunt, or curse, would end in the year 1991. That is exactly 330 years after it had begun. One day, when I was talking with dad about it all, he mentioned to me that when he woke up from the dream he had the night the houses burned, it was 3:30."

Oliver watched his brother's wheels spinning as he laid out his carefully calculated synopsis of events. He was impressed but kept his comments to himself as not to interrupt.

Bret continued, "The two houses burned up in the same way that they used to punish witches back in those days, and so did that odd old lady. I think you are probably right though; she may have already been dead before the fire even started. She was most likely a descendant of one of the families involved in the Great Scottish Witch Hunt."

"I can't believe you figured all of that out by yourself. What do you think it has to do with the woman in the bathtub and the ring?"

"I think Ruth, the old lady next door, was the daughter of the ghost that you saw in the tub. Losing her ring was keeping her from attaining peace of mind, and she had been trapped between worlds since her suicide. We were supposed to help ease her sense of loss by finding her ring. I'm pretty sure that's the meaning of the setting sun reference. It's like ending the last chapter of the story that had started 330 years ago, with her ring representing the closure she needed. We helped her close the circle."

Oliver snatched the book back from Bret's hand. "Let me look at that again."

"You haven't seen anything yet. If you think that's bizarre, just wait till you see this!"

Chapter 6: Precious Dichotomy

Oliver was more than a bit perplexed by the next unexpected thing his brother did. Bret reached up under the bed once again and pulled out another book - it was *The Fellowship of the Ring* - the exact copy that he said he had lost in England. It was the book Oliver had been searching for, and it had been hidden under his bed the whole time. It was tucked up inside his box spring out of sight. Bret had stored it in the one place he knew his brother would never even consider looking.

"I'm glad I waited. I guess I need to practice thinking outside the 'box' more." Both of them laughed.

"Everybody does…if I show you something will you promise on your life not to tell a living soul - at least not yet?"

Oliver made the required promise, and Bret handed him the book.

"Go ahead; open it."

Oliver took the worn copy of *The Fellowship of the Ring* and opened it up apprehensively. Immediately he dropped the book onto the floor with a thud. When it hit the hardwood, out bounced an impressive gold ring with strange markings on it. Oliver plopped down onto his bed with his eyes wide and then reached down to pick up the ring. He was in disbelief, and at that moment even more astounded than he ever could have imagined possible.

Bret began to prepare himself as for how to best convey the story about the mysterious ring to his bewildered brother, and the reason it had come to be pressed beneath the cover of his recently coveted book.

"Wait, is this a trick? I bet you bought this in England at a souvenir shop, and now you are just playing some kind of joke on me."

"Why do you think I left the navy so suddenly? Out of the blue, I came home and went to college to study antiquities; think about it. Did I know you were going to write an essay about this book for your English Lit class? Did I?"

Oliver mumbled to himself, "No…wow, where did this ring come from?"

"What do you know about Roman Mythology?"

"I know more than a little, but not quite enough to know what this is."

"I know you studied Latin in school, but can you make out the inscription on the ring?"

"By the markings on the ring, I can tell it's definitely a Roman artifact. I think it's supposed to say VIVAS IN DEO which would translate to LIVE IN GOD, or something close to that. I'm not sure. It looks to me like the letter 'I' is doubled, and because of that, the O in God is replaced or something. Could it be some kind of spelling mistake, maybe?"

"That's a good guess, and it's also what everyone else seems to think."

"What do you mean – everyone?"

"I discovered something about it nobody else knows yet. You're the first person I've decided to tell since you've practically stumbled right into the middle of things. I don't know what I should do with this ring, but maybe you can help me figure something out. That's why I've kept it hidden here all this time."

Oliver took his eyes off the ring and looked intently at Bret.

"What do you know about it? Tell me."

Bret then asked Oliver if he had heard or read about the Silvianus ring that was found by a farmer while he was plowing a field in Silchester England, in 1785. Oliver said that he hadn't heard of it before. Bret took the ring out of his brother's hand and started telling him the story from the very beginning.

"There was a ring that was stolen from a man named Silvianus while he was bathing at the Roman temple complex in Lydney, near Gloucestershire England, sometime during the 4th century. The thief's name was believed to be Senicianus. This, by the way, is the factual account of the ring that inspired J.R.R. Tolkien to write the books which later became *The Lord of the Rings* trilogy."

"I didn't know anything about that, but I'm confused. What does this ring have to do with it? That story is about a different ring isn't it?"

Bret smiled that confident smile of his and continued as though he were dangling a carrot while tutoring an understudy in antiquities.

"What nobody has ever realized before was that the ring the farmer found in 1785 was only one of two. That's not a doubled 'I,' it's the Roman numeral for two. The inscription wasn't a mistake, it was alphanumeric. This ring is its twin."

Oliver took the ring from his brother's hand and scrutinized it once more.

"That makes a lot of sense, just looking at it with that perspective now."

"There are two almost identical rings. One was forged to represent this material world, and the other to represent the world of the gods. The two rings combined represent the balance of power that governs both the material and ethereal realms. It was almost as though Tolkien had intrinsically honed in on that idea for the basis of his books. This ring, the one that I found, is most likely the second of the two."

"What do you mean the second of the two?"

"I mean it's probably the ring that was created to represent this world, the realm we are presently in. Although the other ring which was sold by the farmer and sat in the library of a country manor for many years collecting dust may very well have been the more powerful of the two. I'm still not quite sure which is which."

"What makes you draw that conclusion?"

"Because in 1888, the same year that Jack the Ripper was wreaking havoc in London, a team of archeologists began excavating the site of the old Nodens Temple. The new owner of the manor where the ring was kept wrote a letter inquiring about its origin. His name was Chaloner Chute.

Ironically, just about that same time, the team of archeologists unearthed a cursed tablet on a place called Dwarf's Hill. It detailed the story of what had happened with the ring that the farmer found."

"How do you know all of this?"

Bret laughed and then chided his brother just a little.

"I finished at the top of my class in military intelligence; remember? I know how to do research. In the process of running all of this historical data down, I also stumbled onto information about Jack the Ripper. He had supposedly removed two brass rings from Annie Chapman's hands. One of the investigating officers named Reid said that the rings had been placed at her feet. I thought it was very odd that all of these things were happening at the same time although they were seemingly unrelated. Now I've forgotten what I was driving at.

Oh yeah, in 1928 that information concerning the two brass rings involving Jack the Ripper was made public in a book written by a guy named, Leonard Matters. It was entitled *The Mystery of Jack the Ripper*. The following year J.R.R. Tolkien consulted on the Roman ring that was found back in 1785 by that farmer in Silchester, regarding its puzzling or coded markings.

I think deep down Tolkien may have somehow intuitively suspected that there was another ring based on its inscription and abnormally large size. I personally believe that it's a reasonable probability that those twin rings belonged to a giant, but as of yet I haven't been able to find any proof to substantiate that theory."

Oliver was hanging on every word and didn't even interrupt his brother's discourse. Bret continued.

"Other archeologists who examined the ring also interpreted VIVAS IN DEO to be misspelled. That's one of the reasons they had asked J.R.R. Tolkien to help out with the etymology of the words inscribed on the ring, but there was no mistake. The inscription was intended to be an alphanumeric code. You are holding the other ring that proves it."

Oliver closed his hand around the ring while he pondered his big brother's intricate tale. He was trying hard to visualize the possibilities of the vast configuration of things based on his own experiences, and what he had just learned about the nature of that fire that had consumed his father's house. Most everyone just assumed that it was a fluke - just another case of bad luck - but both he and his brother knew better.

Chapter 7: The Curse

Oliver sat pensively reflecting as his brother began to regale him with one more enlightening account. Bret recounted the factors that set him on the path which eventually compelled him to visit the place where the Sylvianus Ring had been found. He informed his brother that when he had initially read about the Roman ring that was unearthed in 1785, he realized that the spot was located not too far from where he was stationed at the time. That proximity started him pondering the complexities of the strange artifact, its confusing markings, and abnormally large size.

To Bret, the whole of the backstory was greater than the sum of its parts. He sensed that the ring was more than just ordinary jewelry, worn merely for the purpose of adornment. He immediately considered the possibility that it was intentionally coded and symbolic, and that it also may have inferred physical attributes about the man who wore it.

Bret was convinced that the ring was perhaps a status symbol and a reflection of the individual's ideology. He based that assumption on the fact that it was a signet ring by design with a depiction of the face of the goddess Venus etched into it. That, plus the fact that it was oversized, reinforced his notion that it was worn by a giant. English history, folklore, and legend are riddled with giants, and the more he researched that fact, the more he became convinced he was on the right track.

Bret then informed his brother that the turning point for him to explore the possibility of the existence of another ring came when he read about the supposed misspelling of the Latin phrase inscribed on it. He conceived the idea that it may have been done intentionally. The two juxtaposed I's most likely represented the Roman numeral two as far as he could extrapolate from all of the data which seemed to be painting that picture. At that point, he became fairly confident that there were most likely two rings made, and only one of them had been found.

Bret procured a metal detector and took it to the site of the Roman temple complex at Lydney. He told his brother that he would go there and search inconspicuously for the ring whenever he got free time but came up empty-handed. He unearthed a few other things of interest but not what he was hoping for. So, he changed his strategy and started searching in the same area where the other ring was found in 1785 - Silchester.

As Oliver listened, he began to imagine what he would have done if he had been there, and he broke his long silence by interjecting.

"Wait! Don't tell me; let me guess. When you went there, you strategically picked a place that looked like where the ring might be found. Based on what you knew about the backstory of the other ring, you limited your search grid to a high place. I bet you found it on a hill, where someone who was being pursued might be looking over their shoulder to make sure that they weren't being followed. That's where I would have started looking for it."

"Yes, that's exactly what my strategy was. We do think alike. I went back to the area, digging around for five days off and on. On the 5th day, at dusk, I got a strong signal on the metal detector. I dug down about a foot and a half and pulled up a clump of dirt. I poured the rest of my drinking water onto the small dirt clod and crumbled it between my fingers until I felt something inside. It was the ring you are now holding."

Bret gestured as he looked at his brother, waiting for him to place the ring into his partially cupped hand. He then closed his hand tightly around the heavy gold ring. It was almost as if the memories of everything that had transpired after its discovery began to emanate from it.

"Why did you just hide it here? What do you plan on doing with it?"

Bret pondered his answer carefully. "I really don't know what to do with it. I believe that it is cursed. Maybe both of the rings are, but I'm really not sure."

"You don't believe all that fictional stuff about curses do you?"

"You have no idea what happened to me after I found that ring."

"What happened? Wait, why do you think they are cursed in the first place?"

"Have you ever heard of a defixio? It's an ancient lead tablet with a curse written on it."

"I've never heard that word before."

Bret had scribbled notes about two lead tablets that had been discovered during the excavation of Noden's Temple explaining the nature of the curse he was referring to.

"Listen to this." He picked up his notebook and began to read it aloud.

"FOR THE GOD NODENS, SILVIANUS HAS LOST ONE RING AND DONATED ITS WORTH TO NODENS; AMONG

THOSE NAMED SENICIANUS PERMIT NO GOOD HEALTH – UNTIL IT IS RETURNED TO THE TEMPLE OF NODENS."

Oliver grabbed the notebook from Bret and interjected, "Look, it says one ring, implying that there were two."

"Yes, I noticed that right away, and I postulated that the curse had been invoked by Silvianus after he fell victim to the theft. He subsequently rendered as payment to the Celtic deity Nodens one of the rings – in hopes that the other might be recovered. By entreating Nodens to cause Sencianus to become ill - as punishment for his actions - he attempted to ensure the desired outcome through the wrath of the gods.

I envisioned that Silvianus wore a ring on each hand, one for himself, which was dedicated to his family name, and the other, dedicated to the goddess Venus. When one of the rings was stolen from him by Senicianus, it upset the balance of power that they represented when worn together, and both Silvianus and Nodens sought retribution for the offense. The two rings became a metaphor depicting a mortal being working in concert with a deity to execute their power in the form of a curse."

Oliver said, "Well, if there are two rings, and only one of them is cursed, how do you know which one is?"

Bret seemed to look through him, "I don't know. Maybe both are. On the way back from Silchester the night I found this one I got lost. I wandered pretty much aimlessly in the dark for two hours looking for the road that led back to the train station. I still don't know how I managed to navigate as well as I did.

When I did make it back which should have only taken me a half an hour, I grabbed a ticket and hopped on the train. I had just about an hour left to get back to my flat in London and take a quick shower so I could make it into work on time. The train I was riding on had some kind of breakdown or bomb scare, I never found out what really happened. All of the passengers had to get off at the next station and wait to board another train. The whole thing took 45 more minutes. I ended up being an hour and a half late for work that day."

"So what, that's no big deal. Is it?"

Bret looked down at his shoes, "Normally no, but it turns out that there was a terrorist threat, and London was on high alert. The commander had me discharged from the navy for showing up late for work on that day."

"Wow, I had no idea. So that is the real reason why you left the navy so suddenly and came home."

"Yes, and you're the only one who knows the truth now."

"That doesn't mean the ring is cursed does it?"

Bret replied, "I don't know, but I've never actually put that ring on my finger, and I don't intend to ever do it either."

"I'm not afraid of it!" Oliver snatched the ring from Bret's hand and slipped it over his middle finger before his brother could stop him. Two seconds later there was a loud knock at the front door. Oliver said to Bret, "Hold on, I'll be right back."

He got up and quickly walked out of his room and down the hall. Without warning, the big ring slipped off his finger and hit the floor with a ping. Oliver's eyes followed the ring as it dropped and bounced down the wooden flight of stairs. Shifting his attention from where he was walking for just a second, he stumbled over the lip of the top stair. He slammed his knuckles into the railing as he reached out to grab it to catch himself, but he failed and went tumbling down the entire flight of hard wooden stairs - all thirteen of them. Bret ran out of the bedroom and down the stairs, and he immediately called 911. Oliver was just lying there at the base of the stairs with the ring right beside him. Bret picked up the ring and put it in his pocket - he opened up the door to see who had knocked - but there was no one there. He watched and waited anxiously for the ambulance to arrive while he prayed for a miracle.

The two brothers rode to the emergency room in the ambulance together. Oliver regained consciousness pretty quickly. He had sustained a fractured wrist, and a slight concussion, but he was ok. His ribs were badly bruised as well, but he was thankful to God that it wasn't any worse.

Oliver stayed overnight in the hospital for observation, and Bret returned to his mother's house a few hours later. The next day he picked Oliver up and brought him home. They joked that it was a good thing their mother was out of town for the unexpected excitement. Later that day, Oliver asked Bret if he had put the ring back in the secret place. Bret just winked.

In a concerted effort to solve the dilemma of what to do with the ring, they went back and studied over Bret's notes. They agreed that the curse would most likely be nullified if the ring was returned to the temple of Nodens at Lydney Park in England. Both of them considered taking it back there together and burying it in the ground where it had lain dormant for 16 centuries.

DENOUEMENT

Neither Bret nor Oliver had any intention of handling the ring again. Both were afraid to take it on an airplane with them. The whole time it was under Oliver's bed, it was dormant; he was never even aware of its presence. As a result of that observation, they calculated that the curse didn't apply unless the person in possession of the ring was making physical contact with it.

They realized that it was probably dormant as well when it was in the ground all those years before Bret had disturbed it. When he dug it up and handled it again, they determined that it was reawakened, or reenergized in some way. Putting their heads together, they finally agreed on a plan to rid themselves of the cursed ring once and for all.

Bret still had one good friend left in England that he would talk to once in a while, and he convinced his brother that he could be trusted. The two of them decided to put the ring into a plain brown box with a letter explaining everything, and ship it over to his friend, John Richard Rollins, in London. Then, when they both could get there together, they would visit him and retrieve the ring.

Once they took possession of the ring, they would return it to the old temple of Nodens and bury it several feet deep - well beyond the range of any metal detectors.

Thank you from World Codex staff!
If you enjoyed this 1st book
in the SMR series -
check out Book #2 now available on
Amazon!

OR

If you also enjoy audiobooks -
Sample our breakthrough audio:
Codex SE

Now available on
Amazon, Audible, & iTunes!

SMR Book 2: THE SHOOTING

Codex: Special Edition (audio)

Titanic and Planet Poetry - both seemed doomed from the outset. Why?

www.ingramcontent.com/pod-product-compliance
Lightning Source LLC
Chambersburg PA
CBHW032120280326
41933CB00009B/920